Jesus (Holy Spirit) Is My Ghostwriter!

RAVEN CHASITY ROGERS

Jesus (Holy Spirit) Is My Ghostwriter

Raven Chasity Rogers

Contents

Foreword Minister Damion D. Campbell	xi
Foreword Elder Keith Pierce	xiii

Part 1: The Great Beginning!

Jesus (Holy Spirit) Is My Ghostwriter	3
Get Off Me!	5
I Am B.A.D. (Blessed And Determined)	6
I Do ... If You Do ...	7
A Surprise Found Me In My DM's	8
My Affair With Poetry	9
My Beef With God	10
O' Son-Shine!	12
Sit Back And Watch Me!	13
You Are The King Of My Heart!	14
Reflection	15

Part 2: The Great Middle!

A Friendship So Deep	19
Jaded Spaces	21
Just-In Case	22
O' Wretch-ed One	23
Oh My, Greatness!	24
Safeguard Me!	26
Sister-Girl, Yes, You!	27
So, You Hate Me	29
Unbroken Hope	30
What Do You Think About Me?	31
You No Longer Hurt Me	32
Reflection	33

Part 3: The Great End!

An Invitation, So Tender	37
A Pleasant Reign	38
A Poem Of Salvation	40
BLESSED Sexy!	42
Effervescence of Dreams	43
He's Releasing To Us The W.O.W. (Wealth of Wicked)	44
On Blessed Knee	45
That Same Destination	46
The Greatest Ghostwriter Ever!	47
To My Future	49
You Are The Big-G (God)	50
Reflection	52

Part 4: The Greatest God Ever!

A Light-Yellow House, With A Dark-Gray Door	57
A Scarlet Harvest	59
Black Man, Black King	60
Black Pearl Of Radiance	62
Colorful Thoughts	64
Lavender Love	65
The Blues, I Love	66
Yellow Spring	68
Reflection	69
Acknowledgments	71

If you purchased this book without a cover, you should be aware that this book is stolen property. It was reported as "unsold and destroyed" to the publisher, and the author has not received payment for this "stripped book."

ISBN Number: 0-9960743-7-7 (Paperback)

ISBN Number: 0-9960743–6-0 (E-Book)

LCC Number: 2023912633

Jesus (Holy Spirit) Is My Ghostwriter

Copyright © 2023 Raven Chasity Rogers

Edited by Cynthia M. Portalatín

Published by:

PO Box 1819, Owings Mills, MD 21117

www.maynetre.com

All rights reserved. Except for use in the case of brief quotations embodied in critical articles and reviews, the reproduction or utilization of this work in whole or part in any form by any electronic, digital, mechanical or other means, now known or hereafter invented, including xerography, photocopying, scanning, recording, or any information storage or retrieval system, is forbidden without written prior permission of the author and publisher.

The scanning, uploading, and distribution of this book via the Internet or via any other means without permission of the publisher and author is illegal and punishable by law. Purchase only authorized versions of this book, and do not participate in or encourage electronic piracy of copyrighted materials. Your support of the author's rights is appreciated.

This is a work of fiction. Names, characters, places, and incidents are products of the author's imagination, the author's own personal experience, or are used fictitiously and are not to be construed as real. While the author was inspired in part by actual events, the characters are not distantly inspired by any individual known or unknown to the author. Any resemblance to actual events, locales, business establishments, organizations, or persons, living or dead, is entirely coincidental.

Printed in the United States of America

First Printing 2023

10 9 8 7 6 5 4 3 2 1

Dedication

To the Loving, Masterful and Greatest ghostwriter of all time! Jesus (Holy Spirit)! I wouldn't have it any other way!

Foreword
Minister Damion D. Campbell

Throughout the years, I have always known Raven as a go-getter. We met in church many years ago and have been good friends ever since. She was one who was willing to do things many others around her were not, because she just believed that her God was big enough to do it. We always jokingly called each other "Dr." as a reference to our insatiable hunger of pursuing higher education. Therefore, when she recently made the move to another state and told me she was a published author in less than a year, it was only fitting. Though it was not education that brought her to this point per se; it was once again that willingness to step out on faith in God's Word.

As a prophetic poet myself, when I read her words, I feel both the anointing and the power of her words encouraging, revealing, and reiterating the sentiments of God. It is an edifying experience that generates hope within the heart of the reader. So, it is with great humility and honor that I endorse this great author and her inspiring work.

Foreword
Elder Keith Pierce

I've known Raven for more than 10 years. I've known her to always been kind, considerate and consistent. She is a person who's concerned about family and friends, always advocating and cheering them on to do and be more. Her writing is an extension of her kindness and encouragement.

In 1 Kings 17:4-6 it states "And it shall be, that thou shalt drink of the brook; and I have commanded the ravens to feed thee there. So he went and did according unto the word of the Lord: for he went and dwelt by the brook of Cherith, that is before Jordan. And the ravens brought him bread and flesh in the morning, and bread and flesh in the evening..."

We have all been in a place where it looks like we're in a drought, where we don't know where our next encouraging word will come from. God tells every believer to encourage one another with words of comfort (I Thessalonians 4:18).

Elder Keith Pierce

This book of poetry is God centered to encourage you with words inspired by time spent with God. Words that will help you keep pushing and pursuing your hopes, dreams, and aspirations. The written poems in this book are food that Raven is bringing to you; they will nourish your mind, body and soul.

Part 1: The Great Beginning!

Jesus (Holy Spirit) Is My Ghostwriter
3/3/2023

A pleasant and lovely day readers, whoever you are!
He's so powerful! No introduction needed thus far!
It is plain to see, He's where my help cometh from.
The original ghostwriter, penning these stanzas from day one.
The rules of His writings are an epic game changer.
He blessed the words of each line, to shine brighter. Look out!
DANGER!

Allow me to explain! God Sent the Raven.
The whole time it was Him, giving great words to pen.
There's not a doubt in my mind, just like The Ultimate Homie,
He will always defend!
I couldn't come up with powerful words like this, on the best of my days.
Please let me have the honor to state: it's whatever He says!

He was the Author To My Soul, the whole time; give Him credit!

Raven Chasity Rogers

As I Stargaze upon His marvelous splendor, always! You should have read it!
Every single word written by Him. Many Ventures, that's how I am living and how I got through.
It's okay if you choose to walk in unbelief. Step aside! In faith, I'm believing for you!

Because There's A Story Behind Those Eyes, to tell the truth no retreating!
Dear Blue Skies, will you come out today and give us that beautiful greeting?
Much to prepare, and so much on my mind.
The experience of writer's block, Lord please help! The words I can't find!

You spoke to me saying, Forget Fear! I am with you this day!
To address that Great Commencement, no matter what comes my way.
And like the Invisible Butterfly, it is a challenge to see.
Oh, so speedily, You came up with this masterpiece written for me.

Lord, My Daddy, My Heart, You speak a message to everyone as they flip through the pages.
No discrimination is welcome! Your words of wisdom, a guarantee for all ages.
Now, that the truth is out there and my cover is blown,
I don't care if Home Rejected Me, because Your greatest love sits high on the throne.

Get Off Me!
3/20/2023

Get off me,
with your disrespect.
How dare you mock me
then sit and insult my intellect?
You finally recognize who I am created to be.
And the response to what you see is:
It's not fair! That should be me!
Hush, please! Let me set the record straight!
Get off me! Have a great day, because there's much for me to enjoy on my plate.

I Am B.A.D. (Blessed And Determined)

2/7/2023

I Am B.A.D. to be called by You!
I Am B.A.D. to walk by faith, stand and do!
I Am B.A.D. 'cause Jesus paid a remarkable price!
I Am B.A.D. to live my greatest, blessed life!
I Am B.A.D. to walk in His true, agape love!
I Am B.A.D. by the dopest One from above!
I Am B.A.D. spoken by the Omniscient One!
I Am B.A.D. to live in peace! Now that's fun!
I Am B.A.D. to be the best He set me to be!
I Am B.A.D. chosen by grace so effortlessly!
I Am B.A.D. because He is number One!
I Am B.A.D. to hear Him say, Raven, well done!

I Do ... If You Do ...
11/13/2022

I do, if you do, when ready to conquer the world
I do, if you do, I am not that scared girl
I do, if you do, willing to give us a chance
I do, if you do, will have a beautiful dance!

If you do, I do, will rock with you 'til the end
If you do, I do, will let love be the trend.
If you do, I do, will be your blessing from God
If you do, I do, great things like Moses' rod!

I do ... if you do, will be the best we can be!
Fitly joined together for all to see.

A Surprise Found Me In My DM's
11/13/2022

Eleven-seven was a remarkable and memorable day!
I finally made peace with my past.
That is all I have so kindly to say!
And just like that, a surprising DM at last!

Who would have thought an unexpected DM surprise would cause a shift to take place in my life?
Surprisingly, it found me when I was unaware!
How dare you surprise? That's not fair!

But I'm so excited to know that kindness took the time to send me a DM.
True happiness! Divine!

In an instant, everything has changed!
In an act of faith, I'll never be the same!
Kindness, thank you for that simple request!
Just know I accept and now for the best!

My Affair With Poetry
11/29/2022

At the beginning of our greeting, it seemed like everything that glittered looked just like gold.
Until that one true encounter with poetry got an uninterrupted hold.
A hold of the compassion, by emotionally sharing so many great words.
Words that enabled me to be love stricken, the wisest words ever heard!
A vocabulary of so much goodness had me caught off guard at the time.
Words so pleasantly enticing! Made it difficult to get them off my mind!
Surrounded by the eloquence of your diction.
How can one compare? Is this a fact, or is it fiction?
Made the time spent talking worth every conversation.
I questioned my affair with poetry' was it worth the mention?

My Beef With God
11/24/2022

God, I allowed the frustrations of my heart,
for a short time, to tear our fellowship apart.
My miracle, my blessing was taken from me.
God, I blamed You! What happened? How could this be?
Nine weeks in, no chance of a fight.
Even though my beef with God was real, you still were my light!
Instantly, my heart broke and I felt the pain seep down in my soul.
It hit me by surprise, like the Patriot's comeback at the Super Bowl!
Day after day, living life was a fight!
Sobbing early in the morning when I arose and all over again late at night.
Finally, I understood! I had to repent! I couldn't stay there!
No more questioning God and asking, how come?
Why me? This isn't fair!
My beef with God was a major mistake!

Jesus (Holy Spirit) Is My Ghostwriter

His love held me close and that wasn't fake!
Some time had gone by; I refused to give up and stay down!
The beef I had with God has ceased, and it now rests deep within the ground.

O' Son-Shine!
12/14/2019

Good morning, hello world!
I will shine for you today.
Rise out of bed with good cheer and make the most of this amazing day!
I have the advantage over the dark.
I'll give you direction, when you're lost.
Stop the worrying! Stop the doubting!
I'm always here no matter the cost.
When you look up, I am smiling down.
A ray of hope, for all to see.
As I hover over your face, you will know I am all you need!
So, good morning, hello world!
I will shine for you today.
Move along and live out this journey.
I am here with you always!

Sit Back And Watch Me!
3/3/2023

My purpose He will fulfill!
Sit back and watch me!
Rack up a huge tab.
Don't get angry! Just send Jesus the bill!
My dreams will speak volumes, one by one as they come true!
So glad you treated me like crap.
It's all love! How do you do?
A chosen master of His Agape, while He molds me in the form of His love!
What a pleasant surprise!
You feel me! Gentle as a dove!
Suddenly, my whole life is about to change for the Greater!
Feel free to get your own!
If you refuse, I'm not mad, Love! See you later!

You Are The King Of My Heart!
1/11/2023

Being summoned before Your face, I come humbly before you.
Extraordinary, You are! With no one else to submit to.
Your honor and dignity are what my heart is yielding towards.
Willingly, I submit all that I am, while releasing every cord.
Each and every part of my heart, Your Highness, I lay it gently at your feet.
Invited by the presence of Your power, what a great way to meet!
Empty, I come before the mercy of Your throne.
Symbolizing that sacred place!
Getting pass the nervousness that I'm feeling all over me.
Remaining calm with ease, doing whatever it takes.
No judgment necessary coming from the grace of Your throne.
Your spoken word, spoken over my heart, is a sincere word alone.
With love, You accept even the flawed parts of me, being the King of my heart.
Restoring and releasing me on my way, granting me a refreshing new start!

Reflection

1. Who do you think each poem within the section "The Great Beginning" is written to?
_____
_____
_____
_____
_____

2. What comes to mind as you read each poem in this section?
_____
_____
_____
_____
_____

3. What's your favorite line(s) in each poem within this section?
_____
_____
_____

4. If you had to add another stanza to each poem within this section, what would you write?

Part 2: The Great Middle!

A Friendship So Deep
3/14/2023

Look how far we've come!
Throughout the years, it hasn't been always delightful.
So many challenges we've overcome.
A triumphant reign so bountiful!
From the absolute start, you've given your heart.
At times, I had questioned.
For instance, will this friendship ever grow apart?
Too good to believe that one day we would part ways.
Just to gain a sense of direction and live out these pleasant days.
Our conversations were open, flowing like the water in the sea.
Sometimes, I sit and acknowledge it was God, who sent you to me.
In the past, we were at a distance, but you remained on my mind.
Who would've thought? We'd grow so close,
that I'd hold our friendship like a diamond, a total find.
The gifts of your time and talent I will always treasure.
Your sacrifice is truly genuine! There's no amount of money that could measure.

Raven Chasity Rogers

The richness of your kindness couldn't be discovered within the deepest of oceans.
I enjoy each and every day our friendship is set into motion.
When all is said and done, with many thanks from my heart, I pray our friendship so deep continues to flourish, like it did from the start.

Jaded Spaces
12/26/2022

Here you come again!
Every time I see you I question
the fact that you enable your life to lack luster, and your words
are very faded!
Whenever you enter the room
it's evident! The space immediately becomes jaded!
Please, do the world and yourself a huge favor!
Get a glimpse of reality! Get yourself in order!
Get your luster back and live life with a whole new meaning!
Now, that's major!

Just-In Case
11/22/2022

Just in case you were wondering, Love,
I am full of spectacular surprises.
Who would have thought the love that we share
for each other would leave you fantasizing.

Just in case you need to know,
the love you display towards me will always glow.
Like the brightest light, so illuminating...
to a beautiful paradise is where we're escaping.

Just in case I didn't tell you,
the love you show is impressively remarkable.
No need for an appetite,
just a taste of it and I'm already full!

Just in case, remember this ...
Love, I love you. I love you,
and that will always be true.

O' Wretch-ed One
12/3/2017

O' wretch-ed one! O' wretch-ed one
What is it that you seek after?
Really?! Are you not thankful already?
Everything you need, will come sooner or later
Trust and believe! And you will receive ...

O' wretch-ed one! O' wretch-ed one
Chase after love and it will find you
Have a sincere heart and love will guide you through

With that being said,
everything you'll ever need, you have/possess it!
Don't give up on love!
O' wretch-ed one
You have the right fit ...

Oh My, Greatness!
3/18/2023

Oh my, Greatness!
God, You are at it again.
Allowing me to pen another outstanding poem.
May I begin?

You compose the softness of your word.
Falling fresh upon me, like A Pleasant Reign.
With much to appreciate, Your greatness is evident.
As they Sit Back and Watch Me grow.
I can't complain!

Oh my, Greatness, You demolish the darkness by declaring, O' Son-shine for me today!
In all radiance, and a reminder To My Future, I walk in victory! There's no delay!

To commune, and attached with laughter, we developed A Friendship So Deep.

Jesus (Holy Spirit) Is My Ghostwriter

In Your hand, I present An Invitation So Tender. My heart is yours to keep!
Thank you again as You Safeguard Me with your unfailing presence.
And Just In Case they need to know,
It is to You, I give reverence!

Safeguard Me!
3/11/2011

Safeguard me,
from the cruelty of this world.
Let your Heavenly presence be
my shield.

Your glory alone will safeguard
me and bring hope to my life.
Safeguard my emotions from going
out of control.

Lord, allow the light that You shine down to safeguard me
forever and always!

Sister-Girl, Yes, You!
3/29/2023

A message/poem to the women who have a problem with others thriving... Please get free!

I'm out here living my life while shining
bright for the Son.
You've hated on me, sadly, ever since
the day we were young.
Smiling hard to my face, pretending
that you didn't have a problem.
The mantle skipped you and fell on me,
and your differences appeared all of a sudden.
They say blood is thicker than water.
To me, that's an understatement.
I receive better treatment from a non-
related, total stranger with no resentment.
Sister-Girl, Yes, you! Please go enjoy
your life with some appreciation!
Allow God to have His way in my life!
Calm down! It's not a competition!

Raven Chasity Rogers

Kindly, let the words of this poem, serve
to you as a WARNING!!!
Respect the calling. If you don't, God will
always bless me in your face, and you'll be mourning!
I don't have any problems with you,
as you can see. Go do you! And get free!
With that being said, please enjoy your
life, and allow me to live my BLESSED life and be!

So, You Hate Me
10/16/2019

So, you hate me, because I am beautiful!
So, you hate me, because I am anointed!
So, you hate me, because I am bold!
But you walk around miserable, hateful and cold!

So, you hate me, because I am gifted!
So, you hate me, because I am blessed!
So, you hate me, because you're envious and don't know me!
But your lifestyle mimics the counterfeit you're trying hard to be!

So, you hate me, because I am loved!
So, you hate me, because I am refreshing!
So, you hate me, because my light shines bright!
But you have the nerve to think your hate for me is right!

So, you hate me… Think again, because I am always protected!

Unbroken Hope
3/27/2023

My life has recovered and been restored from a whirlwind of challenges.
Just when I overcame, here it comes
again, another test.
I was able to stand the test of time, because of unbroken hope.
Holding on to the fact that the pieces would come together again.
Yet, I had to allow the healing process to commence, so a new chapter could begin.
Placing all hope in the arms of the true Helper, He granted me life!
The tension around us was much, and can still be cut with a knife.
In fact, that wasn't the lifestyle I wanted to live.
Because there's so much on the inside of me I have to give!
If there's anything I can take away from the message above.
Hold on to the hope that's not broken, and you'll have a better understanding, to walk this life out in love!

What Do You Think About Me?
3/11/2011

What do you think about me?
Do you think I'm charming?
Or friendly?
Am I lazy?

Do I look admirable,
Committed or trustworthy?
Do I show love and affection?
Or a sense of evil in your presence?

If you could ask someone a question,
what would it be?
I would ask, with your honest opinion,
what do you think about me?

You No Longer Hurt Me
12/12/2022

Farewell! Farewell!
Do you comprehend?
You're like the jealous best friend I wished God never sent.
You no longer hurt me with the false hope of your words.
The disrespect of your actions, is the most diabolical ringing sound ever heard!
Unwilling to do right by me,
you're worse than the dust on the shelf.
Go cry somewhere in a corner, and get a firm grip on yourself!

Reflection

1. Who do you think each poem within the section "The Great Middle" is written to?

_____
_____
_____
_____
_____

2. What comes to mind as you read each poem in this section?

_____
_____
_____
_____
_____

3. What's your favorite line(s) in each poem within this section?

_____
_____

4. If you had to add another stanza to each poem within this section, what would you write?

Part 3: The Great End!

An Invitation, So Tender
1/16/2023

From day one, I've invited you into my heart.
My heart, which has been soft and tender.
Tender enough to embrace the emotional and physical part.
The part that left me rejected, I had to render.
Render by releasing my pureness.
The pureness of the radiant innocence of heart.
An innocence of heart, that had me feeling guilty.
Yet, I had to ponder!
Ponder on the simple fact, that now I must try to justify.
Justify the sense of accepting it was not your fault!
No fault of yours, because of my willing invitation to you.
It was to you I gave the serenity of my heart.
My heart that you've taken for granted.
For granted, but I live to grow!
Now, you've been forgiven!
Forgiven to the point where you can no longer press on my heart, because I've invited peace to come instead!

A Pleasant Reign
3/17/2023

Lord. Outpour upon me Your presence on another level.
Not a drip, but a gush of Your majestic power.
Shower down; let it bevel!
Your majesty, rule and reign over my life from an angelic presence so pleasant.
Enrich my soul with your kingdom glory.
Uplifting, yet so reverent.
Fervently, I need more than a sprinkle.
Depict my life. Please RESTORE!!

A Pleasant Reign, embraced like an inheritance I didn't deserve.
In honor of this opportunity, to You, let me serve!
Hallelujah! Hallelujah! Hallelujah! It is so!
Shield my heart with Your majesty.
Let Your compassion for love overflow.
Confront and illuminate me daily as I seek for Your direction.
Your dialogue spoken to me is my utmost protection.

Jesus (Holy Spirit) Is My Ghostwriter

Endow the fulfillment and instill Your Pleasant Reign down in my soul.
Flooding the capacity of my life. Wherever,
You lead me to go.

A Poem Of Salvation
3/27/2023

Today is the right day to be set free.
Confess with your mouth and believe
in your heart, the Lord Jesus,
so that your soul may live with Him in eternity.
He is waiting to receive you! Love,
with open arms.
Be not afraid! Come forward, my child, there
is no need to be alarmed.
The price for your sins has already
been paid on Calvary.
Hallelujah! Thank you, Jesus!
For giving us the VICTORY!!!

Romans 10:8-10 (King James Version)
8 But what saith it? The word is nigh thee, even in thy mouth, and in thy heart: that is, the word of faith, which we preach;
9 That if thou shalt confess with thy mouth the Lord Jesus, and shalt believe in thine heart that God hath raised him from the dead, thou shalt be saved.

Jesus (Holy Spirit) Is My Ghostwriter

10 For with the heart man believeth unto righteousness; and with the mouth confession is made unto salvation.

BLESSED Sexy!
2/5/2023

Anointed, compassionate and special in your sight.
I am amazing, strong and given the power to fight.
Here's a new term that will surely make your day.
The words are BLESSED SEXY and are here to stay!
That's right! Yeah, I said it! Here it is! Yup, it's true!
Shower down from the high throne to shape its form in the new.

BLESSED SEXY to be chosen from my mother's womb.
BLESSED SEXY from the one who created the stars, sun and moon.
BLESSED SEXY when I walk in His grace with liberty.
BLESSED SEXY because His dear Son died for you and died for me.
BLESSED SEXY being grateful, while receiving His very best!
BLESSED SEXY stepping into that Holy glow, nothing else to say. You get the rest!

Effervescence of Dreams
3/8/2023

An inspiration to the life I have been gifted,
to leap over walls.
Walking with the approval of God, to thrive higher.
I don't seek after your applause.
A major discovery for unbelievers within close range or afar.
The effervescence of beautiful dreams forming from above as the morning star.
Coming true with elegance, like a flowing gown, worn gracefully on the red carpet.
You're welcome to present the beauty of your splendor.
It's a feeling of déjà vu! Got me saying, have we ever met?

He's Releasing To Us The W.O.W. (Wealth of Wicked)

3/28/2023

We've waited a long time, for a divine
moment like this!
To open up to receive a W.O.W. type of blessing, that is so bliss!
A guarantee in His word, spoken to the masses
who are the just and believe!
An outpouring of the W.O.W. blessings being released, leaving
us so relieved!
Time and time again, they refuse to get it right in their hearts.
To receive an understanding, of Who it came from, and that's
where it starts.
Here comes blessing after blessing, rushing down!
It's here at last!
Taken from their hands and into our possession.
Supernatural W.O.W. blessings! Now, that is fast!

On Blessed Knee
3/20/2023

You awaken me with a thirst and a yearning to see what today will be.
Coming humbly before You, with singing on my lips, while down on blessed knee.
Surrendering all my struggles and happiness before Your remarkable throne.
I'm reminded by You, throughout the day, that I am NEVER alone.
A complete zeal for the purpose set before me, to live out each and every day.
On blessed knee, awaiting instruction.
Nevertheless, to You I pray.
Without Your word, I don't have the light afforded for me to see.
That's why daily I must take the time to seek You, kneeling down on blessed knee.

That Same Destination
3/26/2023

Seconds, minutes, hours, days, weeks, months, years, and miles apart.
For some, an unpleasant road trip, but where do we start?
To end up at that same destination, we have to set aside some time to get there.
Nevertheless, every obstacle is not without reason.
In regards to life, it's still our year!
To arrive at the same destination assigned from God, who will come through in a different method.
It's amazing to discover, that how we get there is the result of how we were tested.
A mindful discovery and experience will be well-worth the adventure.
Pushing past, walking by faith, just to avoid that painful lecture.
Escaping every distraction, with the powers to renew your mind!
So, when we arrive at that same destination, rewarding blessings we shall find!

The Greatest Ghostwriter Ever!
3/29/2023

Extremely incredible! Allow me to help y'all get acquainted.
To the readers, who don't know, Jesus
(Holy Spirit) is My Ghostwriter.
His words are NEVER tainted.
A satisfaction to attest, He is magnificent at what He does.
If you have an issue with this statement, go ahead, put on the gloves!
Let me warn you now! His word will hit you hard, leaving you seeing and thinking Colorful Thoughts.
No worries! He is forgiving! Just like A Poem Of Salvation, it is okay! It's not your fault!
Now, let us move this poem along. Jesus is a loving God! Don't you see?
Showering down like a Pleasant Reign, endless possibilities!
It is significant! He loves us so, because He is The King Of My Heart!
To solidify by making all things new,
So, we don't grow apart.

Blessed Sexy are His ways, because He is the best and the greatest!
The word of God is the gospel of good news, no need to wait for the latest.
For instance, Black Man, Black King, He will supply all of your needs.
By sending you a Black Pearl Of Radiance to be fruitful with while multiplying your seeds!
While enjoying life and spreading hope, and so much of Lavender Love, to appreciate all things that were created.
Oh My, Greatness! The Great One from above.

To My Future
6/12/2017

To my future ...
I want to taste the love (that flows) flowing on my tongue.
Sounds of joy, love and compassion
springing forth like water, refreshing to my soul.

As I look into your eyes,
I can see,
and with your touch
I can feel, my life beginning to blossom.

With the past left behind me and
the present wide open, I must appreciate it!
Before, I meet the gift of my future, I find out
I am destined for greatness.

And the taste of love flowing on my tongue, will bless me with possibilities so endless.

XOXO ... My Destiny!

You Are The Big-G (God)
3/30/2023

Revealing all possibilities around the world and throughout this beautiful nation.
With You, Big-G, all things are made good, because there's no need for an explanation.
Majestically, everything is created by the power of Your voice and spoken into existence.
Leaving a hypnotic surprise to everyone engaging, while watching the great performance.
The beauty of the seasons exists, like the flowers blooming during the peaceful Yellow Spring.
A time so celebratory and well-appreciated like the woman who is wearing the expensive diamond ring.
God, Your love never fails, and You don't make any mistakes.
Some should NEVER refer to You as little-g, cause You're a Big-G, who NEVER leaves nor forsakes.
Gifting us a confidence to enhance in this journey.
The Unbroken Hope in you, springs from a well deep inside me.

Jesus (Holy Spirit) Is My Ghostwriter

Big-G, You are the greatest beacon of light, shining down, for all to see!

And the best carpenter to ever build, A Light-Yellow House With A Dark-Gray Door that's strategically crafted for me.

Reflection

1. Who do you think each poem within the section "The Great End" is written to?

_____
_____
_____
_____
_____

2. What comes to mind as you read each poem in this section?

_____
_____
_____
_____
_____

3. What's your favorite line(s) in each poem within this section?

_____
_____

Jesus (Holy Spirit) Is My Ghostwriter

_____
_____
_____

4. If you had to add another stanza to each poem within this section, what would you write?

_____
_____
_____
_____
_____

Part 4: The Greatest God Ever!

A Light-Yellow House, With A Dark-Gray Door
3/26/2023

888 square feet of a solid foundation and a triple-new beginning.
Every obstacle we were faced with to overcome was worth the winning.
A craftsman-style home with light-yellow siding had been spoken into existence.

As you walk to the front door, dark-gray in color, open with persistence.
Inside you will see, according to the floor plan presented, three bedrooms soon ready for decor.
So ready to embrace the promise by enjoying, shouting and singing praises that will soar.

It's the powerful number three, representing Holy Trinity, the ultimate powers that be!
A love given to us so patiently, pouring down on you and on me.

Enabling this gift shared between the two of us, making this house a home.

Suddenly, that light-yellow house with the dark-gray door is now here for us to own.

A Scarlet Harvest
3/18/2023

His blood protects my harvest from the fountain tongue of your weak language.
A solace, being covered by the power of His scarlet blood, is a gift and a privilege.
Shattering every weapon at your disposal,
you're already facing defeat!
I do not wrestle against flesh and blood, 'cause
I relinquish all of my cares at his feet.
The crops and my harvest, are not affected by your weakness and your vain glory.
After all, I overcome by the blood of the Lamb, and the words of my blessed true story!

Black Man, Black King
3/17/2023

Black man, Black king!
Do you know who you are?
You're one of God's blessed creations, who bring about joy.
Stand with power! Unite in your kingship, and begin to enjoy!
The present of life has been gifted and set before you since the beginning of time.
A time of conquest, where you have been called to invade all territories belonging to you.
Therefore, possess the riches God purposed for you to inherit, and leave an unforgettable mark worth looking forward too.

Black man, Black king!
Walk there-in, standing tall, marked for generations and generations to see and know, He didn't allow you to fall.
Surrounded and covered by Almighty God to arise and take your place on the throne.
Fear not! You're going to rise above the ashes, if you have to embrace the title alone.
It's okay! The Lord is with you.

Jesus (Holy Spirit) Is My Ghostwriter

So, wear that crown with dignity.
Capture every moment with thanksgiving and let the melody of
each victory be spent marching in liberty.

Black man, Black king
You are a jewel to the world!
So precious, yet endowed with valor, gifted to the young boy
and girl.
Now, fight with guidance and accept to reign
in the position.
And trust and know that He will renew, restore and gracefully
help you complete the mission.

Black man, Black king
powerful are the words that you speak.
So profound to many of them, that you will teach.
A divine platform, that your feet will be set upon.
To engage as the influencer and connect through outreach.
And, finally, your legacy is waiting on you to be the Black man,
Black king, God has sought out for you to be.

Black Pearl Of Radiance
3/25/2023

Perfected and shielded with a flawless melanin coating, quite astonishing, I'm sure!
The UV rays of sunshine given enhance one to explore.
Handcrafted in different colors, shades and
sizes – embodied to be loved.
The authenticity of the black pearl, an insightful piece and one of a kind, cannot be shoved.
In its rarest form, too diligent, an imitator cannot compare.
The beauty of a black pearl so radiant, one will say; so envious, it really is not fair!
A sparkling result, brightly shining from a distance, yet hidden away for a specific time.
I am so thankful to be one of them, a justly fortune, rightfully mine!
From the ancestors of past generations, equipped and strong women glazed by the glow.
The footprints of their triumphant victories have been planted upon all of us to grow.

Jesus (Holy Spirit) Is My Ghostwriter

Ladies, black pearls of radiance, with open arms embrace that you are different! This is you!
And don't ever embellish the birth right that is yours for the taking. Genuinely, this you do!

Colorful Thoughts
3/18/2023

Leave it to my vivid imagination, and what do you get?
A mind of luminous colors and that's where my thoughts are set.
A clearance of gratitude to appreciate the brightness occurring in retina display.
A depiction of green trees, yellow sunflowers, red roses, and the awesome flying blue jay.
An exquisite treasure seen and well-worth the find.
Every color, unique in its own right, and for that, I don't mind!
The dwelling place to my natural habitat, with different shades galore.
Fresh colors striking the blank canvas, now that, I do adore!
A new way to think with great capability, Your divine color scheme grabs my attention.
Needless to say, an extravagant piece of artwork develops, with an extraordinary outcome surely worth the mention.

Lavender Love
3/18/2023

Can't you tell at this point, that I'm a blessed romantic?
Obviously, if you saw what I've been through, you'll know why, it's not magic!
Colors seem to bring out the best love and joy all around us.
Let me acknowledge the fact: the visual effects of it are a bonus!
Lavender is a beautiful color! What's not there about it to love?
It sparks a joy on the inside, that can only come from Heaven above.
A display of grace and serenity, that's how I desire my love life to be.
To walk with a calm sense of elegance. The way God intends for it to be.
The dynamics of this color are worth every dividend and all royalties.
Lavender love hold close to me, defining all of the remarkable abilities!

The Blues, I Love
3/14/2023

Overcome with calmness, by the variety of your color pallet made available to me; sing to me harmoniously without permission to be.
Sky blue, make yourself available today, for all the world to see. As I place my eyes, looking up to you, taking it all in so graciously.

Turquoise, do you realize how relieving you are?
It's my pleasure to attest, you're incredibly one of my favorite colors thus far.
Simply, I am enlightened by the scheme of your color, and can identify it from afar.

Royal blue, give me a moment! Where do I begin?
You enable the deity of your richness to sing something new.
Oh, how I appreciate the beautiful sentiments that I get from you.
Your melodious majesty is there seeing me all the way through.

Jesus (Holy Spirit) Is My Ghostwriter

I create a smile, when I witness your color coming into full view.

Navy blue, let us not give this meeting a second chance.
The true importance and power of your time is not happenstance.
Let me be direct by asking, when you get a chance,
may I be the one to have the first and only dance?

Yellow Spring
3/24/2023

Sunflowers, yellow Lillie's and sunshine galore.
It is Springtime! Everyone, listen up! There are fun times in store.
Eating hotdogs from the hotdog stand, adding mustard on them, you know what's up.
Lemonade refreshing and cold to drink, let me have a large one and fill the cup!
A yellow blimp flying high, kissing up to the clear blue sky.
Watching the dog chase after the yellow frisbee, as I am gladly walking by.
Yellow canaries singing sweet music leaving a gentle fragrance in the air.
I am overjoyed with so much cheer! Springtime, it's my favorite season of the year.

Reflection

1. Who do you think each poem within the section "The Greatest God Ever" is written to?

_____
_____
_____
_____
_____

2. What comes to mind as you read each poem in this section?

_____
_____
_____
_____
_____

3. What's your favorite line(s) in each poem within this section?

_____
_____

_____
_____
_____

4. If you had to add another stanza to each poem within this section, what would you write?

_____
_____
_____
_____
_____

Acknowledgments

Special thanks to my Ultimate best friend, Lord and Savior, for blessing me with gumption and wit to write another blessed and powerful book, for all to enjoy.

To my compassionate and loving father, Mr. Roy Rogers, for his generosity, time and support towards the gifts that God placed inside of me. To the entire Rogers' family, near and far. I love y'all so very much! To my amazing siblings, thank you always, but a special thanks to my little sister Robyn and little brother Rory. Thank y'all for the sweet laughs, while showing true support! A special shout out to Minister Damion Campbell, for speaking life to me through encouraging words and blessed intercession. To Maynetre Manuscripts, LLC, thank you dearly for helping to bring this vision to pass.

To a dear friend, Sister Betty for providing honest feedback, while supporting my craft. Shout out to Bazier Taylor and Yojarlin, for being true examples of good friends! I pray all the best for y'all! And a great appreciation to the beautiful pastor, who God used to send me His message pertaining to this gift of writing poetry, a sincere thanks! Lastly, to everyone near and far, whoever spoke or showed me love throughout the years, a heartfelt thank you, to you all!

www.ingramcontent.com/pod-product-compliance
Lightning Source LLC
LaVergne TN
LVHW051510070426
835507LV00022B/3029